In the Power of His Might

Workshop Workbook

Introduction to

EFFECTIVE SPIRITUAL WARFARE

Charles Pretlow

In the Power of His Might
Introduction to Effective Spiritual Warfare
WORKSHOP WORKBOOK

May 2015
Copyright © Charles Pretlow

All rights reserved. Printed in the United States of America. No part of this publication may be reproduced, stored in a retrieval system, or transmitted, in any form or by any means electronic, mechanical, photocopying, recording, or otherwise, without the prior written permission of the author.

Unless otherwise indicated, all Scripture quotations are from the Holy Bible, English Standard Version ® (ESV®), copyright © 2001 by Crossway, a publishing ministry of Good Publishers. Used by permission. All rights reserved.

ISBN 978-1-943412-02-0

Published by -
Wilderness Voice Publishing, LLC
Canon City, Colorado USA
www.wvpbooks.com

In the Power of His Might
Introduction to
Effective Spiritual Warfare
Workshop Workbook

Dear Participant:

God's people must learn and then become trained in prosecuting effective spiritual warfare. Our foe and his minions are strong, pervasive, and humanly unmatched; however, if we walk in the power of God's might we will be victorious. Like David, we can be accurate and deadly with our prayers and our battles against the giants who work in the powers of darkness. This is the main objective of this workshop, to introduce the sincere disciple of Christ to our Lord's training and discipline in this most important contest of faith.

Your interest in entering into spiritual combat against the powers of darkness and prayerfully watching in intercession for the will of God to be done is very commendable. However, every sincere Christian should be instructed on the importance of effective spiritual warfare where God's perfect will is executed by His power and not in one's our own carnal spiritual power.

There are many pitfalls to be avoided and solid Biblical principles to understand in the process of becoming a weapon in God's hands. Most importantly, we must learn how to allow the true Christ to be formed within us—that we know Him and he knows us, as we continually abide in Christ.

This workshop will introduce you to those challenges in spiritual warfare often overlooked or misunderstood and that will minimize the suffering involved in taking on the devil and exposing the ground he unrightfully stands upon.

True spiritual warfare will be difficult and become increasingly intense in the coming days. As the end of this age approaches, every Christian will be thrown headlong into a universal spiritual battle where destruction awaits the unprepared, the naïve, the untrained and the arrogant believer. Satan and his minions are experts at deception and the use of evil people and even carnally driven Christians who often unknowingly become his pawns in the fight to prayerfully see God's will come to fruition.

So buckle your belts and become attentive to this series of lectures where Biblical principles and case studies will help you grasp what it takes to be effective for the Lord in wrestling against the evil powers of this present darkness.

May you be led and empowered by his Spirit,
MC Chapel Fellowship Team

Workshop Format and Rules

Welcome to this important workshop, we appreciate your interest and attendance. The format is lecture orientated to include scripture exhortation and Biblical principle explanations with some case studies. Each session will last approximately forty-five minutes with a 15 minute break between each, having a ninety minute lunch break after the third session.

Since the subject matter is intense and requires attentiveness, distractions such as comments (pro or con) during presentations will not be allowed, but can be presented during the Q&A session. Cell phones and pagers are to be turned off or set to silent mode.

The subject of spiritual warfare, deliverance, and casting out the demonic (exorcism) is not new. However, the need to dismiss myths and false teachings on these important topics is of the utmost importance. Much of the material presented today will be new to some of you. For those who have studied and worked in a spiritual warfare and deliverance ministry, some of what you hear may not agree what you have been taught or even experienced. If this is the case, we recommend patiently attending the whole workshop presentation and hold your questions and comments for the question and answer period.

Thank you for your courteous participation.

Table of Content

Day One

Session 1: Understanding the Enemy's Power — 6

Session 2: The Full Armor of God — 11

Session 3: Principalities and Demons — 16

Session 4: Evil, the Human Spirit, and Cohabitation — 21

Session 5: Question and Answer Session — 26

Day Two

Session 6: Finger of God Power and Prayer — 28

Appendix: Becoming a Weapon in God's Hands — 29

In the Power of His Might Workshop   Date:____/____/_____   Presenter:_____

SESSION ONE   SLIDE ONE
Understanding the Enemy's Power

- **A Quantum Shift in Spiritual Warfare Thinking**
- **Powers of Darkness Promoting a Different Gospel**
- **Naiveté and Deception:** *2 Corinthians 11:12-15*
    - **Case of the Exploding Glass of Milk**
    - **Case of the Demonic Funnel-Tunnel**
    - **Case of the Angel-of-Light Visitation**

Key Points:
- The emphasis of spiritual warfare has been upon fighting the powers of darkness to take back America from secularism, socialism, abortion on demand, and LGBT culture and upon trying to restore prayer in school, Christ in Christmas, and Family wholesomeness at the Magic Kingdom (Disney Land).
- Leadership fell asleep at the wheel and drove God's people into the ditch as angel-of-light false leaders hijacked the Gospel of Christ.

Notes:

_____

_____

_____

_____

_____

_____

_____

Learn how to contend against darkness in the true power of Christ!

SESSION ONE — SLIDE TWO
Understanding the Enemy's Power

- **Satanic Strong Holds - Defilements Hidden Within**
- **Casting Out Carnality and Double Mindedness?**
- **Passivity, Magic Thinking, and Symptom Suppression**
- **Satan Plays Possum**
- **Mental Illness and the Demonic**

Key Points:
- A truncated anti-cross Gospel has lulled millions of Christians into a passive and careless approach in dealing with the powers of darkness and evil implants.
- Quick fix gimmicks and carnal spiritualism is prevalent in most deliverance ministries, setting up believers to buy into the devil's bait and switch program.
- Sweeping the house clean is a false deliverance scam, leaving the passive and defiled Christian vulnerable and defenseless to future demonic attacks.
- A wounded/crushed spirit and damaged emotions classified as mental illness often allows the demonic to cohabitate.

Notes:

_____
_____
_____
_____
_____
_____
_____

SESSION ONE — SLIDE THREE
Understanding the Enemy's Power

- **Exposing Darkness:** *Ephesians 5:11-21*
- **Evil Veiled in a Cloak of Decency**
    - **Holding the Form of Godliness:** *Romans 16:17-20*
    - **Good Outer Persona - Evil Inner Core**
- **Jesus Taught and Trained the Disciples**
    - **Few Enter into Christ's School of Ministry**

Key Points:
- Part of the mission of every saint is to prayerfully expose hidden evils, in fellowship and within the society they live in. This can be a challenge, for Satan will oppose these efforts.
- Evil is more common than ever and is cloaked in decency hidden from the naive Christian.
- Evil people exist and are Satan's pawns and workers.
- There is a process of training that every saint must endure; however, few know how to embrace and endure this training and discipline.

Notes:

Learn how to contend against darkness in the true power of Christ!

SESSION ONE — SLIDE FOUR
Understanding the Enemy's Power

- **Satan's Power to Hide and Deceive**
  - Few Mature in Discernment and Alertness
    - A Roaring lion: *1 Peter 5:8-11*
  - Most live on the Milk of the Word
- **Lack of Training – Lack of Suffering:** *1 Peter 5:9*
- **Poorly Trained Faculties:** *Hebrews 5:11-14*
- **Few have Christ Within.** *1 John 4:4, Galatians 4:19*

Key Points:
- Satan's power to deceive, hide, and counterfeit must be overcome by the sincere saint. The devil paints himself as harmless, on the run, and a fraidy-cat, when in reality he is a vicious lion who devours the naive and the sleeping.
- The milk of the Word of God is well known, yet few have their powers of discernment trained where the meat of the Word becomes life changing and lifesaving.
- Three main keys are being in Christ, walking in His fullness within, and dying to conjuring up carnal spiritualism as a substitute.

Notes:

In the Power of His Might Workshop   Date:____/____/____   Presenter:_____

15 Minute Break

More Space for Notes:

_____

_____

_____

_____

_____

_____

_____

_____

_____

_____

_____

_____

_____

_____

_____

_____

_____

_____

Learn how to contend against darkness in the true power of Christ!

SESSION TWO — SLIDE ONE
The Full Armor of God

- **Spiritual Forces of Evil – No Laughing Matter**
  - *Ephesians 6:10-20*
- **Paul's Metaphor - Military Combat Protection**
- <u>Whole</u> **Armor - The Necessity of Understanding**
- **The Key is in Christ – and in the Power of His Might**
  - Sons of Sceva Syndrome: *Acts 19:11-20*

Key Points:
- As the end of this age unfolds, Scripture clearly describes and warns that the devil and his minions will exercise great power with signs, wonders, and evil powers to destroy.
- As Christians we must understand fully how to walk in God's protection (His whole armor) and stand in his power against the spiritual forces of darkness.
- Many Christians take for granted the power of Christ that is available and use his name haphazardly.
- Satan has learned to play possum with the naïve and the arrogant, setting many up to fall when the battles become intense.

Notes:
_____
_____
_____
_____
_____
_____
_____

SESSION TWO   SLIDE TWO
The Full Armor of God

- **The Whole Armor of God Metaphor Explained:**
  - Must Put on the Whole Armor that God has Provided
  - Therefore Stand, (Don't Run in the Face of the Enemy)
  - Truth is our Core Strength (Denial and Self-deception)
  - Righteousness from a Pure Heart (Hidden Defilements)
  - Proper Footing - Peace (Anger of Man will Sabotage)
  - True Faith in Christ (Not in Self or in Carnal methods)

Key Points:
  - Magically chanting to put on the full armor of God is absolutely ludicrous and invites eventual disaster.
  - Each piece of military armor covers vital parts of the body. The Apostle explains that the Christ-like attributes of truth, righteousness, etc. are vital to have within our being - and not to be pretended.

Notes:

Learn how to contend against darkness in the true power of Christ!

SESSION TWO   SLIDE THREE
The Full Armor of God

- **Explanation of Metaphor Continued:**
  - **Understanding Salvation (Working it out for Real)**
  - **Sword of the Spirit (Offensive Weapon)**
    - **The Rhema Word (Scripture Applied by the Spirit)**
  - **Prayers led and Inspired by the Holy Spirit—Always**
    - **A Steady Prayer Life of Intercession that is Heard from on High!**
  - **Be Alert and Persevere in Suffering (Not Passive/Rote)**
  - **Boldness in the Spirit—Not Carnal Arrogance**

Key Points:
  - Christians are to work out their own salvation and grow up into Christ. Many try take on Satan's territory in immaturity and in their own spiritual power.
  - Passivity, impurities of heart, a double-minded condition, and carnal energy when doing spiritual warfare is like trying to put out a fire with a can of gasoline.

Notes:

In the Power of His Might Workshop   Date:_____/_____/_____   Presenter:_____

SESSION TWO SLIDE FOUR
The Full Armor of God

- **Soldiers of Christ — Discipline and the Work of the Cross**
    - **Many Christians are AWOL**
    - **Passivity and the Cares of this Life**
    - **Secret Sin and Carnal Motives**
    - **Patient Endurance.**
    - **Dying to the Spiritual Power of the Flesh.**

Key Points:
- The work of the cross in the believer's life is often misunderstood, yet it is vital when working with Christ in His training and discipline.
- In Christ's army, as in any military, one cannot do their own thing. Leaving one's post when on guard duty is a serious offence. Likewise, not embracing our cross and dying to our own agenda may cause severe trouble.
- Christ warned that many who have practiced spiritual warfare apart from Christ's leadership and direction will not be able to enter eternity. Jesus referred to such as lawless, whom he never knew.

Notes:

_____
_____
_____
_____
_____
_____
_____
_____

Learn how to contend against darkness in the true power of Christ!

15 Minute Break

More Space for Notes:

SESSION THREE — SLIDE ONE

Principalities and Demons

- **Spiritual Rulers - Fallen Angels**
  - Most are Ignorant of Satan's Designs: *2 Corinthians 2:11*
  - They Affect, Manipulate, and Control
  - They use Humans—and the Human Spirit
  - They use Carnal and False Christians
- **They Create and Perpetuate Archetype Thinking**
  - Elemental Spirits: *Colossians 2:6-23*
  - Gripping the Free Will and the Unconscious Mind
  - False Doctrine Based on out of Context Truth

Key Points:
- Understanding the nature and intentions of the rulers of darkness and the god of this world is very important in every aspect of life on earth. It is paramount that we as servants of Christ not be found ignorant of Satan's schemes, methods, or how and who he uses as his servants.

Notes:

_____
_____
_____
_____
_____
_____
_____

Learn how to contend against darkness in the true power of Christ!

SESSION THREE — SLIDE TWO
Principalities and Demons

- **Examples of Archetype beliefs:**
  - Relationship Idolatry
  - Homosexuality as a Mistake in Gender at Birth
  - Racial Prejudice and Opposite Gender Judgments
  - Extraterrestrials and Evolution
- **Angel of Light Principalities and Archetype Thinking**
  - Manifesting False Signs and Wonders
  - Promote Leadership Idolatry
  - Develop False Teachings that Produce Carnal Spiritualism
  - Churchianity – the Worship of Fellowship

Key Points:
- Principalities are fallen angels that hold great spiritual power and influence by inspiring and perpetuating myths, faulty logic, lies, and Bible truths taken out of context as well as demonstrate false signs and wonders along with counterfeit gifts.

Notes:

SESSION THREE   SLIDE THREE
Principalities and Demons

- **Demons are Agents of the Devil and the Fallen Angels**
- **Demons Work with and within a Human's Being or Spirit**
  - **Influence and Latch onto Wounds and Defilements to the Human Spirit**
  - **Can Oppress, Possess, and Cohabitate**
  - **Double Minded Condition — (Crushed Spirit and Damaged Emotions)**
- **Making a Clean Slate or Becoming Religious does not Remove Demonic Strongholds:** *Matthew 12:43-45*

Key Points:
- Demons are subordinate to the fallen angels (principalities or spiritual rulers of darkness). Some noted theologians believe demons are those beings cast into darkness who died in the great flood.
- Demons look for the personal spirit of defiled humans to live within.

Notes:

_____
_____
_____
_____
_____
_____
_____

Learn how to contend against darkness in the true power of Christ!

SESSION THREE SLIDE FOUR
Principalities and Demons

- **Demons can be Identified throughout Scripture:**
  - Unclean spirit, spirit of infirmity, an Evil Spirit
  - Demonic Spirits Associate with the Works of the Flesh
    - Spirit of Sorcery—a Power Demon
    - Spirit of Jealousy, Contention, Strife, etc.
- **Demons can Work, Oppress, Cohabitate**
  - Within Christians who are Carnal, who Practice Sin, or who are Double Minded
- **Purify the Heart and Cleanse Defilements of Body/Spirit.**
  - *James 4:7-10, 2 Corinthians 1:1*

Key Points:
- Demons latch onto carnal Christians who still suffer from latent defilements to the spirit and impurities of the heart.
- Double minded Christians (divided in soul and crushed in spirit) can have multiple demonic access points and can even have demons cohabitate in dividedness.

Notes:

In the Power of His Might Workshop   Date:_____/_____/_____   Presenter:_____

Lunch Break 12 PM to 1:30 PM

More Space for Notes:

Learn how to contend against darkness in the true power of Christ!

SESSION FOUR — SLIDE ONE
Evil, the Human Spirit, and Cohabitation

- **Not all have Faith;** *2 Thessalonians 3:1-5*
- **Over the Top Last Days Evils**
- **Evil and Unbelieving Heart of the Carnal Christian.**
  - Serious Problem: *Hebrews 3:12-15*
  - The Case of the Unbelieving Father / Pastor
- **And One of You is a Devil:** *John 6:60-71*
- **Weeds, Waterless Springs — Accursed Children**
  - Parable of the Weeds: *Matthew 13:24-43*
  - Peter's Exhortation: *2 Peter 2:12-22*

Key Points:
- Last days evil will grow in an exponential manner and evil people will go from bad to worse. Satan will use implants amongst God's people as he did with the disciples when he used Judas to do the unthinkable.
- A vital part of spiritual warfare is distinguishing good from evil and discerning the evil person disguised as a good person or even a good Christian.

Notes:

SESSION FOUR   SLIDE TWO
Evil, the Human Spirit, and Cohabitation

- **Most Insidious Work of the Devil and Evil**
  - **Enlisting the Human Spirit to Wage Battle**
  - **Carnal Spiritualism's Power – Even Over Demons**
    - *Matthew 7:21-23*
- **Exposing Darkness:** *Ephesians 5:11*
  - **Searing One's own Conscience:** *1 Timothy 1:18-20*
  - **Self-induced Amnesia (Believing One's own Lies)**
  - **The Case of the Church Picnic Predator**

Key Points:
- Controlling and using the human spirit is one of the devil's most masterful achievements, in culture and within carnal and apostate Christianity.
- People who succumb to doing evil do so by rejecting conscience and developing the ability to lie and then believe their own lie. These are the devil's implants throughout the world and within the Christian community.

Notes:

_____
_____
_____
_____
_____
_____
_____

Learn how to contend against darkness in the true power of Christ!

SESSION FOUR — SLIDE THREE
Evil, the Human Spirit, and Cohabitation

- **Out-of-Body Spirit Travel**
  - **Misinterpretation of the Apostle Paul's Notice**
    - *1 Corinthians 5:3-5*
- **End of the Age Evils — Demons Manifesting**
  - **Idolatry, Worship of Demons, Sorcery, Murder...**
    - *Revelations 9:20-21*
- **Lust for Spiritual Power - Spiritual Power of Man**
  - **Counterfeit Power Demon Invades**

Key Points:
- The human spirit is dead to God until regeneration by the Holy Spirit and acceptance of Christ as Lord and Savior. However, the human spirit can be activated by Satan through forbidden practices, defilements, and abuse.
- False doctrine can defile a Christian's personal spirit whereby it can be invaded by counterfeiting demons.
- False manifestations and carnal spiritualism within Charismatic and Pentecostal fellowship become haunts for counterfeiting power demons.

Notes:

_____
_____
_____
_____
_____

SESSION FOUR   SLIDE FOUR
Evil, the Human Spirit, and Cohabitation

- **Double Minded Madness — Split in the Core**
  - **A Double Heart:** *Psalm 12:2*
  - **Demonic Cohabitation — a Judas heart**
  - **Satan Enters and Fills the Heart of the Wicked**
    - *Luke 22:3 and Acts 5:3*
- **False Deliverance**
  - **Cannot Cast Out Double Mindedness or a Divided Core**
- **God's Recovery Program Found in the Book of James**
  - **Resist the Devil, Draw Near to God**
  - **Stop Sinning, Purify the Heart, Recover from Dividedness**

Key Points:
- The book of James explains the characteristics and symptoms of a double minded condition.
- Some people are divided in spirit and soul, and even become split in the heart (core) and allow the demonic to live freely within and give the right Satan to fill their hearts.

Notes:

_____
_____
_____
_____
_____
_____
_____

Learn how to contend against darkness in the true power of Christ!

15 Minute Break

More Space for Notes:

In the Power of His Might Workshop   Date:____/____/____   Presenter:_____

SESSION FIVE SLIDE ONE
Review w/ Questions and Answers

More Space for Notes:

Learn how to contend against darkness in the true power of Christ!

SESSION FIVE — SLIDE ONE
Review w/ Questions and Answers

More Space for Notes:

Session Six — Slide One
Finger of God Power and Prayer

- **The Sufferings of Christ:** *Galatians 6:1-10*
  - Standing in the Gap and Burden Bearing
- **Apart from Christ** – *we can do nothing*
- **In His Power and in His Protection**
  - A process of Picking up our Cross Daily
- **In the name of Christ, in Christ, by Knowing Christ**
- **Effectual and Fervent Prayer:** *Acts 12:5-11*
  - In His Righteousness, in the Holy Spirit
- **For Healing, for Exposing Darkness, for Confronting Evil**
  - The case of the handcuffed stalker: *Acts 13:4-13*

Key Points:
- Battling the forces of darkness involves suffering. As servants of Christ we must understand what it means to fulfill the law of Christ in doing battle.
- Using the name of Christ without truly knowing Christ is asking for trouble.
- Effective prayer requires sincerity and a righteousness that is genuine.

Notes:

_____
_____
_____
_____
_____
_____
_____

Learn how to contend against darkness in the true power of Christ!

Appendix
Becoming a Weapon in God's Hands

The end of this age is roaring towards us and God's people, for the most part, are passive—asleep just as Christ forewarned in Scripture—in particular the parable of the Ten Maidens. (See Matthew 25:1-13.)

Now is the time to give Christ permission to deal with you in any and all ways necessary to bring you to a place of preparedness. Each of us must become disciplined, trained, and transformed to where the fullness of Christ can be ours.

It is Christ in us, in the form of Christ-like character and the fullness of the Holy Spirit that will get us through the coming dark and difficult days. We cannot make ourselves into a true servant of Christ, where God can use us effectively in battle. Only by His hand in life's trials and circumstances, along with our cooperation, can we become mature in Christ. God is faithful to transform us as we embrace each challenging moment eager to dye to our agenda, have out carnal motives exposed, while allowing the Holy Spirit to bring newness of life. *"And we all, with unveiled face, beholding the glory of the Lord, are being transformed into the same image from one degree of glory to another. For this comes from the Lord who is the Spirit"* (2 Corinthians 3:18).

We must learn to allow Him to transform us and refrain for reprogramming ourselves using religious self-powered methods.

It is the discipline of the Lord as described in Hebrews chapter 12 that will produce holiness, strength, and wisdom that will make us into a weapon God can use against the forces of darkness.

Enlist now in God's army, where His training will be tough, challenging, and thorough that you may be made perfect, complete, and lack nothing.

May God richly bless you as you give Him permission to transform you.

MC Chapel Fellowship Team

www.ingramcontent.com/pod-product-compliance
Lightning Source LLC
Chambersburg PA
CBHW081357040426
42451CB00017B/3484